TREASURE
for a
SISTER'S HEART

TREASURES FOR A SISTER'S HEART

Compiled by Karey Hoff

Copyright © 1996 by Garborg's Heart 'n Home, Inc.

Published by Garborg's Heart 'n Home, Inc.
P. O. Box 20132, Bloomington, MN 55420

Except for Scripture verses, masculine pronouns have been replaced with gender neutral or feminine pronouns to personalize the quotes for sisters like you.

SPCN 5-5044-0270-0

$\mathcal{M}$ay God's richest blessings be upon you both today and throughout the year–and may those blessings flow through you to touch the lives of everyone you meet.

GARY SMALLEY

JANUARY 1

*I*f we celebrate the years
behind us they become
stepping stones of strength
and joy for the years ahead.

DECEMBER 31

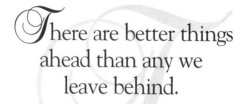

There are better things
ahead than any we
leave behind.

C. S. LEWIS

JANUARY 2

$\mathcal{M}$ay the Lord
continually bless you
with heaven's blessings as
well as with human joys.

PSALM 128:5 TLB

DECEMBER 30

I don't dream of wealth and success for you. But instead, a job you like, skills you can perfect, enthusiasms to lighten your heart, friends, and love in abundance.

PAM BROWN

JANUARY 3

Never be afraid to trust an unknown future to an all-knowing God.

❧

CORRIE TEN BOOM

DECEMBER 29

$\mathcal{W}$hat lies behind us,
and what lies before us are
tiny matters, compared to
what lies within us.

RALPH WALDO EMERSON

JANUARY 4

I will honor Christmas in my heart and try to keep it all year.

CHARLES DICKENS

DECEMBER 28

$\mathcal{T}$wo are better than one, because they have a good reward for their toil. For if they fall, one will lift up the other.

❧

ECCLESIASTES 4:9,10 NRSV

JANUARY 5

*R*ecall it as often as you wish, a happy memory never wears out.

❧

LIBBIE FUDIM

DECEMBER 27

What do we live for, if not to make the world less difficult for each other?

GEORGE ELIOT

JANUARY 6

Christ is the still point of the turning world.

T. S. ELIOT

DECEMBER 26

$\mathcal{W}$e may give without loving, but we cannot love without giving.

JANUARY 7

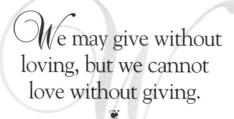

*F*or to us a child is born, to us a son is given, and the government will be on his shoulders. And he will be called Wonderful Counselor, Mighty God, Everlasting Father, Prince of Peace.

ISAIAH 9:6 NIV

DECEMBER 25

*T*hough we travel the world over to find what is beautiful, we must carry it within us or we find it not.

❦

JANUARY 8

God grant you the light in Christmas, which is faith; the warmth of Christmas, which is love...the all of Christmas, which is Christ.

WILDA ENGLISH

DECEMBER 24

*B*e kind to one another, tenderhearted, forgiving each other, just as God has forgiven you.

EPHESIANS 4:32 TLB

JANUARY 9

*G*od became a man. While the creatures of earth walked unaware, Divinity arrived. Heaven opened herself and placed her most precious one in a human womb.

MAX LUCADO

DECEMBER 23

$\mathcal{S}$o much of what
we learn of love we
learn at home.

❧

JANUARY 10

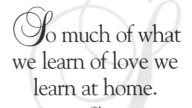

*C*hristmas is
the celebration of the
keeping of a promise....
A saving promise.

MICHAEL CARD

DECEMBER 22

The highest love of
all finds its fulfillment
not in what it keeps,
but in what it gives.

FATHER ANDREW SDC

JANUARY 11

*B*ehold, a virgin shall be with child, and shall bring forth a son, and they shall call his name Emmanuel...God with us.

Matthew 1:23 KJV

DECEMBER 21

*Y*our truest friend is
the one who is a friend
without expecting
anything in return.

JANUARY 12

To receive a gift, molded from love and sacrifice, selected with care and tied up with all the excitement the giver has to offer, is indeed rare. They don't come along often, but when they do, cherish them.

ERMA BOMBECK

DECEMBER 20

*W*hen a sister asks,
there is no tomorrow.

JANUARY 13

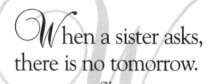

*C*hristmas, my child, is love in action.... Every time we love, every time we give, it's Christmas.

DALE EVANS ROGERS

DECEMBER 19

$\mathcal{T}$he earth is filled
with his tender love

PSALM 33:5 TLB

JANUARY 14

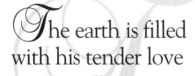

$\mathcal{L}$ove.... It comes out
of heaven, unasked
and unsought.

PEARL S. BUCK

DECEMBER 18

*L*ove, like sunshine's warmth, beams forth on every side and bends to every need.

❦

JANUARY 15

*I*t is good to be children sometimes, and never better than at Christmas, when its mighty Founder was a child himself.

CHARLES DICKENS

DECEMBER 17

Happy times and bygone
days are never lost.... In truth,
they grow more wonderful within
the heart that keeps them.

❧

KAY ANDREW

JANUARY 16

*H*ow great is the love the Father has lavished on us, that we should be called the children of God. And that is what we are!

1 JOHN 3:1 NIV

DECEMBER 16

When you were born,
God said, "Yes!"

JANUARY 17

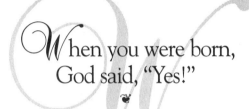

*G*od is so big He can cover the whole world with His love, and so small He can curl up inside your heart.

JUNE MASTERS BACHER

DECEMBER 15

*I*t isn't the big pleasures that count the most; it's making a great deal out of the little ones.

JEAN WEBSTER

JANUARY 18

*L*ove has its source in God, for love is the very essence of His being.

KAY ARTHUR

DECEMBER 14

A friend loveth
at all times.

PROVERBS 17:17 KJV

JANUARY 19

*D*elight yourself in the surprises of today!

DECEMBER 13

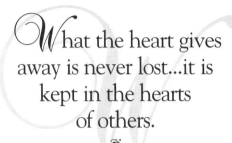

$\mathcal{W}$hat the heart gives
away is never lost...it is
kept in the hearts
of others.

❧

JANUARY 20

It is the season to be jolly because, more than at any other time, we think of Jesus. More than in any other season, His name is on our lips.

MAX LUCADO

DECEMBER 12

There will be days which are great and everything goes as planned. There will be other days when we aren't sure why we got out of bed. Regardless of which day it is, we can be assured that God takes care of our daily needs.

EMILIE BARNES

JANUARY 21

My God is changeless in his love for me.

PSALM 59:10 TLB

DECEMBER 11

She who wishes to secure
the good of others has
already secured her own.

❦

JANUARY 22

The time to be happy
is now; the place to
be happy is here.

❦

ROBERT G. INGERSOLL

DECEMBER 10

*Y*ou are tenderly
loved by the One
who created you.

❧

JANUARY 23

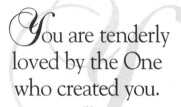

$\mathcal{G}$od knows the rhythm of my spirit and knows my heart thoughts. He is as close as breathing.

DECEMBER 9

$\mathcal{M}$ay you always be doing those good, kind things which show you are a child of God, for this will bring much praise and glory to the Lord.

PHILIPPIANS 1:11 TLB

JANUARY 24

There is no substitute
for plain, everyday
goodness.

MALTBIE D. BABCOCK

DECEMBER 8

There is no limit
to the power of a
good woman.

R. H. BENSON

JANUARY 25

Every good and perfect gift is from above, coming down from the Father of the heavenly lights, who does not change like shifting shadows.

JAMES 1:17 NIV

DECEMBER 7

$\mathscr{B}$eauty does not come with creams and lotions. God can give us beauty, but whether that beauty remains or changes is determined by our thoughts and deeds.

DELORES DEL RIO

JANUARY 26

*L*ove sacrifices all things to bless the thing it loves.

LORD LYTTON

DECEMBER 6

*L*ove grows by giving. The love we give away is the only love we keep. The only way to retain love is to give it away.

❧

JANUARY 27

*S*isters believe in
your dreams as much
as you do.

❧

DECEMBER 5

$\mathcal{B}$lessed are they who can laugh at themselves, for they shall never cease to be amused.

❧

JANUARY 28

$\mathscr{P}$eace is not a season,
it is a way of life.

❧

DECEMBER 4

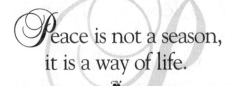

$\mathcal{M}$y children, we should love people not only with words and talk, but by our actions and true caring.

1 JOHN 3:18 NRSV

JANUARY 29

*G*od will never let you
be shaken or moved
from your place near
His heart.

JONI EARECKSON TADA

DECEMBER 3

$\mathcal{W}$e would worry less
about what others think
of us if we realized
how seldom they do.

❧

ETHEL BERRETT

JANUARY 30

Thanks be to God for his indescribable gift!

2 CORINTHIANS 9:15 NIV

DECEMBER 2

$\mathcal{A}$ sister is one who knows you as you really are, understands where you've been, accepts who you've become, and still gently invites you to grow.

JANUARY 31

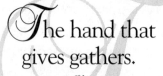

The hand that gives gathers.

ENGLISH PROVERB

DECEMBER 1

$\mathcal{T}$here is no pleasure in having nothing to do; the fun is in having lots to do and not doing it!

❧

MARY LITTLE

FEBRUARY 1

*H*appiness is being at peace; being with loved ones; being comfortable.... But most of all, it's having those loved ones.

❧

JOHNNY CASH

NOVEMBER 30

*T*hose who bring
sunshine into the lives
of others cannot help but
keep it from themselves.

❧

SIR JAMES M. BARRIE

FEBRUARY 2

Faith expects from
God what is beyond
all expectation.

ANDREW MURRAY

NOVEMBER 29

Above all, love each other deeply, because love covers a multitude of sins.

1 PETER 4:8 NIV

FEBRUARY 3

*Every day shared
with the ones we love
is a gift for which we
are very thankful!*

NOVEMBER 28

Time has a wonderful way of showing us what really matters.

FEBRUARY 4

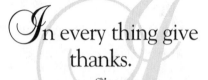

In every thing give thanks.

1 THESSALONIANS 5:18 KJV

NOVEMBER 27

*H*e cannot bless us unless He has us.... In love, He claims all.

C. S. Lewis

FEBRUARY 5

*T*hanksgiving is a time of quiet reflection upon the past and an annual reminder that God has, again, been ever so faithful. The solid and simple things of life are brought into clear focus.

❧

CHARLES R. SWINDOLL

NOVEMBER 26

*W*hat the heart has
once owned and had,
it shall never lose.

HENRY WARD BEECHER

FEBRUARY 6

There's always something
for which to be thankful.

CHARLES DICKENS

NOVEMBER 25

$\mathcal{A}$t the end of your life you will never regret not having passed one more test, not winning one more verdict, or not closing one more deal. You will regret time not spent with a husband, a sister, a child, or a parent.

BARBARA BUSH

FEBRUARY 7

To be grateful is to recognize the love of God in everything He has given us— and He has given us everything. Every breath we draw is a gift of His love, every moment of existence a gift of grace.

THOMAS MERTON

NOVEMBER 24

The Lord is good to those whose hope is in him, to the one who seeks him; it is good to wait quietly for the salvation of the Lord.

LAMENTATIONS 3:25-26 NIV

FEBRUARY 8

Thank the Lord for his steadfast love, for his wonderful works to humankind. For he satisfies the thirsty, and the hungry he fills with good things.

PSALM 107:8,9 NRSV

NOVEMBER 23

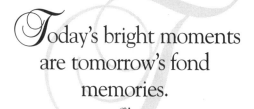

Today's bright moments
are tomorrow's fond
memories.

❧

FEBRUARY 9

Gratitude. More aware of what you have than what you don't. Recognizing the treasure in the simple— a child's hug, fertile soil, a golden sunset. Relishing in the comfort of the common.

MAX LUCADO

NOVEMBER 22

*O*ne can never consent
to creep when one feels
an impulse to soar.

HELEN KELLER

FEBRUARY 10

*S*eeing our Father in everything makes life one long thanksgiving and gives a rest of heart.

HANNAH WHITALL SMITH

NOVEMBER 21

$\mathcal{W}$e have been in God's
thought from all eternity,
and in His creative love, His
attention never leaves us.

MICHAEL QUOIST

FEBRUARY 11

Our love is the unfolding
miracle that expands
our joy.

ALLA BOZARTH-CAMPBELL, PH.D.

NOVEMBER 20

People are like stained-glass windows; they sparkle and shine when the sun is out, but when the darkness sets in their true beauty is revealed only if there is a light within.

ELIZABETH KUBLER-ROSS

FEBRUARY 12

Thank God for regular days. There are far too few of them.

GLORIA GAITHER

NOVEMBER 19

If one falls down, his friend can help him up.

❦

ECCLESIASTES 4:10 NIV

FEBRUARY 13

*G*ive thanks to the Lord,
for he is good; his love
and his kindness go
on forever.

1 CHRONICLES 16:34 TLB

NOVEMBER 18

$\mathcal{L}$ife is the childhood
of immortality.

DANIEL A. POLING

FEBRUARY 14

The glory of friendship is...the spiritual inspiration that comes to one when they discover that someone else believes in them and is willing to trust them with their friendship.

RALPH WALDO EMERSON

NOVEMBER 17

*O*ur joy will be complete if we remain in His love—for His love is personal, intimate, real, living, delicate, faithful love.

MOTHER TERESA

FEBRUARY 15

*H*appiness always looks small while you hold it in your hands, but let it go, and you learn at once how big and precious it is.

NOVEMBER 16

It is good to let a little sunshine out as well as in.

FEBRUARY 16

Good friends are good forgivers.

NOVEMBER 15

The older you get the more you realize that kindness is synonymous with happiness.

LIONEL BARRYMORE

FEBRUARY 17

*E*very morning tell him,
"Thank you for your kindness,"
and every evening rejoice in
all his faithfulness.

PSALM 92:2 TLB

NOVEMBER 14

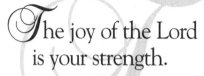

The joy of the Lord
is your strength.

NEHEMIAH 8:10 TLB

FEBRUARY 18

*L*ove has a short memory. It needs continual reminders.

LARRY CHRISTENSON

NOVEMBER 13

Know that you yourself are a miracle.

DR. NORMAN VINCENT PEALE

FEBRUARY 19

*L*ove makes burdens lighter, because you divide them. It makes joys more intense, because you share them. It makes you stronger, so that you can reach out and become involved with life in ways you dared not risk alone.

NOVEMBER 12

*B*lessed are those who can give without remembering, and take without forgetting.

ELIZABETH BIBESCO

FEBRUARY 20

A sister is someone who knows all about you, and still chooses not to go away.

NOVEMBER 11

*R*eal generosity is doing
something nice for someone
who'll never find it out.

FRANK A. CLARK

FEBRUARY 21

$\mathcal{T}$ake time to laugh, it is the music of the soul.

NOVEMBER 10

It is one of the beautiful compensations of this life that no person can sincerely try to help another person without also helping himself.

RALPH WALDO EMERSON

FEBRUARY 22

$\mathcal{M}$y Presence will go
with you, and I will
give you rest.

EXODUS 33:14 NIV

NOVEMBER 9

$\mathcal{I}$ will trust and not be afraid, for the Lord is my strength and my song; he is my salvation.

ISAIAH 12:2 TLB

FEBRUARY 23

*G*od not only knows us, but He values us highly in spite of all He knows. "You are worth more than many sparrows . . . ." You and I are the creatures He prizes above the rest of His creation.

❧

JOHN FISCHER

NOVEMBER 8

The best memory is that which forgets nothing but injuries. Write kindnesses in marble and write injuries in the dust.

❧

PERSIAN PROVERB

FEBRUARY 24

The more one learns
to live, the more one
learns to live without.

❧

NOVEMBER 7

$\mathcal{E}$verything you do is a portrait of yourself.

FEBRUARY 25

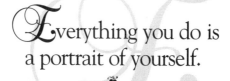

*G*ood communication
is as stimulating as
black coffee, and just
as hard to sleep after.

ANNE MORROW LINDBERGH

NOVEMBER 6

*H*appiness is found
along the way, not at the
end of the journey.

❧

FEBRUARY 26

The Lord has done great things for us, and we are filled with joy.

PSALM 126:3 NIV

NOVEMBER 5

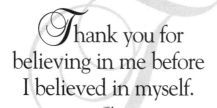

*T*hank you for
believing in me before
I believed in myself.

❧

FEBRUARY 27

$\mathscr{T}$hose who dare to ask anything of a friend, by their very request seem to imply that they would do anything for the sake of that friend.

CICERO

NOVEMBER 4

A cheerful heart
is good medicine.

PROVERBS 17:22 NIV

FEBRUARY 28

*M*y sister hears the song in my heart and sings it to me when my memory fails.

NOVEMBER 3

*M*ay the warming love of friends
surround you as you go,
Down the path of light and laughter
where the happy memories grow.

HELEN LOWRIE MARSHALL

FEBRUARY 29

He made you so you
could share in His creation,
could love and laugh
and know Him.

❧

TED GRIFFEN

NOVEMBER 2

A sister listens to your deepest hurts and feels they are hers too.

❦

MARCH 1

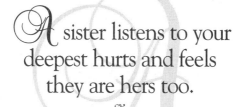

$\mathcal{M}$ay God be gracious to us and bless us and make his face shine upon us.

PSALM 67:1 NIV

NOVEMBER 1

Things turn out
best for the people who
make the best of the
way things turn out.

ART LINKLETTER

MARCH 2

Goodness is the only
investment that
never fails.

❧

HENRY DAVID THOREAU

OCTOBER 31

The guardian angels of life
sometimes fly so high as to be
beyond our sight, but they are
always looking down upon us.

❦

JEAN PAUL RICHTER

MARCH 3

$\mathcal{G}$od is not too great to
be concerned about
our smallest wishes.

❧

BASILEA SCHLINK

OCTOBER 30

I am still confident in this:
I will see the goodness of the Lord
in the land of the living. Wait
for the Lord; be strong and take
heart and wait for the Lord.

PSALM 27:13,14 NIV

MARCH 4

The next best thing
to being wise oneself is
to live in a circle of
those who are.

❧

C. S. LEWIS

OCTOBER 29

$\mathscr{L}$ove loves to be told
what it knows already....
It wants to be asked for
what it longs to give.

❧

P. T. FORSYTH

MARCH 5

$\mathscr{G}$etting things accomplished
isn't nearly as important
as taking time for love.

❧

JANETTE OKE

OCTOBER 28

The best way to cheer yourself up is to try to cheer somebody else up.

MARK TWAIN

MARCH 6

*C*hoose for yourselves this day who you will serve.... As for me and my house, we will serve the Lord.

JOSHUA 24:15

OCTOBER 27

$\mathcal{C}$ontentment is not the fulfillment of what you want, but the realization of how much you already have.

❧

MARCH 7

*S*isters have one
soul between them.

❧

OCTOBER 26

*I*t is love which gives things their value.

❧

C. CARRETTO

MARCH 8

$\mathcal{W}$e are so very rich
if we know just a few
people in a way in which
we know no others.

CATHERINE BRAMWELL-BOOTH

OCTOBER 25

They that wait upon the Lord shall renew their strength. They shall mount up with wings like eagles; they shall run and not be weary; they shall walk and not be faint.

ISAIAH 40:31 KJV

MARCH 9

*H*ow others treat us
will make little difference
when we know we have
God's approval.

OCTOBER 24

*H*appy is the one
who has learned to hold
the things of this world
with a loose grip.

❧

MARCH 10

$\mathcal{W}$e know that in all things God works for the good of those who love him.

ROMANS 8:28 NIV

OCTOBER 23

$\mathcal{Y}$our greatest pleasure
is that which rebounds
from hearts that you
have made glad.

❧

HENRY WARD BEECHER

MARCH 11

*B*esides the noble art of getting things done, there is the noble art of leaving things undone. The wisdom of life consists in the elimination of nonessentials.

OCTOBER 22

*H*appiness is a perfume
you cannot pour on
others without getting
a few drops on yourself.

RALPH WALDO EMERSON

MARCH 12

*D*o not forget little kindnesses, and do not remember small faults.

CHINESE PROVERB

OCTOBER 21

*O*ur love to God is
reflected in the love we
have for one another.

❧

MARCH 13

*O*riginality is not doing something no one else has ever done, but doing what has been done countless times with new life, new breath.

MARIE CHAPIAN

OCTOBER 20

*B*ut now the
Lord who created you
says...I have called you by
name; you are mine.

ISAIAH 43:1 TLB

MARCH 14

How beautiful a day can be when kindness touches it.

GEORGE ALLISTON

OCTOBER 19

True happiness consists
not in the multitude
of friends, but in the
worth and choice.

BEN JONSON

MARCH 15

$\mathcal{L}$ove comes from God
and those who are loving
and kind show that they
are the children of God.

1 JOHN 4:7 TLB

OCTOBER 18

*G*o to the effort. Invest the time. Write the letter. Make the apology. Take the trip. Purchase the gift. Do it. The seized opportunity renders joy.

❧

MAX LUCADO

MARCH 16

*L*ove is giving freely,
expecting nothing
in return.

❧

MARY CARSON

OCTOBER 17

The real joy of life is in its play. Play is anything we do for the joy and love of doing it.

WALTER RAUSCHENBUSCH

MARCH 17

The secret of life is that all that we have and are is a gift of grace to be shared.

LLOYD JOHN OGILVIE

OCTOBER 16

*H*appy is the man who knows
what to remember of the past,
what to enjoy in the present, and
what to plan for the future.

❧

A. GLASON

MARCH 18

*Y*ou cannot step
twice into the same river,
for other waters are
continually flowing on.

❧

HERICLITUS

OCTOBER 15

*H*e surrounds me
with lovingkindness and
tender mercies. He fills
my life with good things.

❧

PSALM 103:4,5 TLB

MARCH 19

*L*ord, you have examined
my heart and know everything
about me.... You both precede and
follow me, and place your hand of
blessing on my head.

PSALM 139:1,5 TLB

OCTOBER 14

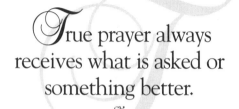

$\mathcal{T}$rue prayer always
receives what is asked or
something better.

MARCH 20

I have held many things in my hands, and I have lost them all; but whatever I have placed in God's hands, that I still possess.

MARTIN LUTHER

OCTOBER 13

Oh, the comfort, the
inexpressible comfort of feeling
safe with a person: having neither
to weigh thoughts nor measure
words, but to pour them out.

GEORGE ELIOT

MARCH 21

I find that as I grow older, I love those most whom I loved first.

THOMAS JEFFERSON

OCTOBER 12

True friends are those seeking solitude together.

ABEL BONNARD

MARCH 22

The most wonderful flattery is to let a person talk on and to simply listen.

OCTOBER 11

$\mathcal{T}$his is the day the Lord has made. We will rejoice and be glad in it.

PSALM 118:24 TLB

MARCH 23

*I*f you treat an individual as
if she were what she ought to be
and could be, she will become what
she ought to be and could be.

❦

OCTOBER 10

I believe in the sun even when it is not shining. I believe in love even when I do not feel it. I believe in God even when He is silent.

❦

MARCH 24

If you give, you will get! Your
gift will return to you in full and
overflowing measure, pressed down,
shaken together to make room
for more, and running over.

LUKE 6:38 TLB

OCTOBER 9

*G*od delights to meet the faith of one who looks up to Him and says, "Lord, You know that I cannot do this...but I believe that You can!"

AMY CARMICHAEL

MARCH 25

Nobody has ever measured, even poets, how much a heart can hold.

ZELDA FITZGERALD

OCTOBER 8

God's fingers can touch nothing but to mold it into loveliness.

❦

GEORGE MACDONALD

MARCH 26

Putting an emotion into words gives it a life and a reality that otherwise it doesn't have.... Similarly, expressing confidence in a person's ability to accomplish something actually strengthens that ability.

ARTHUR GORDON

OCTOBER 7

God understands our prayers even when we can't find the words to say them.

MARCH 27

Today, see if you can stretch your heart and expand your love so that it touches not only those to whom you can give it easily, but also those who need it so much.

DAPHNE ROSE KINGMA

OCTOBER 6

*P*eople worry and God smiles.

HEBREW PROVERB

MARCH 28

In quietness and trust
shall be your strength.

Isaiah 30:15 NIV

OCTOBER 5

*H*ow precious it is, Lord, to realize that you are thinking about me constantly! I can't even count how many times a day your thoughts turn towards me.

PSALM 139:17 TLB

MARCH 29

When we allow God the privilege of shaping our lives, we discover new depths of purpose and meaning.

JONI EARECKSON TADA

OCTOBER 4

$\mathcal{W}$e do not understand the intricate pattern of the stars in their courses, but we know that He who created them does, and that just as surely as He guides them, He is charting a safe course for us.

BILLY GRAHAM

MARCH 30

$\mathcal{I}$t is the simple things of life that make living worthwhile, the sweet fundamental things such as love and duty, work and rest, and living close to nature.

LAURA INGALLS WILDER

OCTOBER 3

As Jesus stepped into the garden,
you were in His prayers. As Jesus looked
into heaven, you were in His vision.... His
final prayer was about you. His final pain
was for you. His final passion was you.

MAX LUCADO

MARCH 31

Sisters are the chocolate chips in the cookie of life!

❧

OCTOBER 2

$\mathcal{T}$hank you, Father, for the beautiful surprises you are planning for me today. So often in my life...an unexpected burst of golden sunshine has exploded through a black cloud, sending inspiring shafts of warm, beautiful sunshine into my life.

ROBERT SCHULLER

APRIL 1

*Y*ou created my inmost being;
you knit me together in my mother's
womb. I praise you because I am fearfully
and wonderfully made; your works are
wonderful, I know that full well.

❧

PSALM 139:13,14 NIV

OCTOBER 1

*G*od loves each one
of us as if there
were only one of us.

❧

AUGUSTINE

APRIL 2

A friend is one to whom one may pour out all the contents of one's heart, chaff and grain together, knowing that gentle hands will take and sift it, keep what is worth keeping, and with a breath of kindness, blow the rest away.

GEORGE ELIOT

SEPTEMBER 30

God has made His children by adoption nearer to himself than the angels.

THOMAS WATSON

APRIL 3

$\mathcal{E}$very day in a life
fills the whole life with
expectation and memory.

C. S. LEWIS

SEPTEMBER 29

I will not forget you.
See, I have inscribed you
on the palms of my hands.

ISAIAH 49:15,16 NRSV

APRIL 4

A smile costs nothing but gives much. It takes but a moment, but the memory of it sometimes lasts forever.

❧

SEPTEMBER 28

God's forgiveness and love exist for you as if you were the only person on earth.

CECIL OSBORNE

APRIL 5

I will lie down and sleep in peace, for you alone, O Lord, make me dwell in safety.

❧

PSALM 4:8 NIV

SEPTEMBER 27

$\mathcal{T}$o love someone
is to look into the
face of God.

❧

APRIL 6

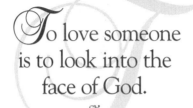

$\mathcal{L}$ove has been called the most
effective motivational force in all the
world. When love is at work in us, it is
remarkable how giving and forgiving,
understanding and tolerant we can be.

CHARLES R. SWINDOLL

SEPTEMBER 26

*J*esus cannot forget us; we have been graven on the palms of His hands.

❦

LOIS PICILLO

APRIL 7

*O*ccupy a small space
in a great way.

❧

SEPTEMBER 25

*B*lue skies with white clouds on summer days. A myriad of stars on clear moonlit nights.... Bluebirds and laughter and sunshine and Easter. See how He loves us!

ALICE CHAPIN

APRIL 8

*G*ood company on a
journey makes the
way to seem all
the shorter.

❧

IZAAK WALTON

SEPTEMBER 24

*H*e who began a good work in you will carry it on to completion until the day of Christ Jesus.

PHILIPPIANS 1:6 NIV

APRIL 9

There is a blessing in my life that keeps repeating...you, you, you, you, you!

ROY LESSIN

SEPTEMBER 23

*L*ove is the reason behind everything God does.

APRIL 10

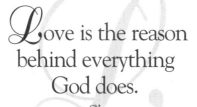

*M*ay the Lord watch
between you and me
when we are absent
one from another.

GENESIS 31:49 NKJV

SEPTEMBER 22

Among God's best gifts to us are the people who love us. The great acts of love are done by those who are habitually performing small acts of kindness.

APRIL 11

There is no joy like
the joy of sharing.

❦

BILLY GRAHAM

SEPTEMBER 21

$\mathscr{T}$hough our feelings come and go, God's love for us does not.

C. S. LEWIS

APRIL 12

$\mathcal{M}$ay God send His love like sunshine in His warm and gentle way, to fill each corner of your heart each moment of today.

❦

SEPTEMBER 20

*S*ome people make
the world special just
by being in it.

❦

APRIL 13

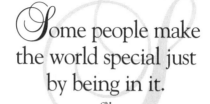

*L*ove feels no burden,
thinks nothing of trouble,
attempts what is above its
strength, pleads no excuse
of impossibility.

❧

THOMAS À KEMPIS

SEPTEMBER 19

As far as God is concerned, there is a sweet, wholesome fragrance in our lives. It is the fragrance of Christ within us.

2 CORINTHIANS 2:15 TLB

APRIL 14

*E*ncourage each other to build each other up, just as you are already doing.

1 THESSALONIANS 5:11 TLB

SEPTEMBER 18

If it weren't for the
last minute, nothing
would get done!

APRIL 15

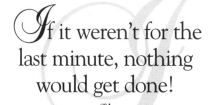

*S*ilences make the real
conversations between friends.
Not the saying, but the never
needing to say is what counts.

❧

MARGARET LEE RUNBECK

SEPTEMBER 17

*L*ove is the expansion of two natures in such fashion that each includes the other, each is enriched by the other.

FELIX ADLER

APRIL 16

$\mathcal{B}$e patient with yourself and others. Growing fruit takes time.

❧

SEPTEMBER 16

*E*very time we
encourage someone,
we give them a
transfusion of courage.

CHARLES R. SWINDOLL

APRIL 17

The best friendships have weathered misunderstandings and trying times. One of the secrets of a good relationship is the ability to accept the storms.

ALAN LOY McGINNIS

SEPTEMBER 15

*R*each out and care for someone
who needs the touch of hospitality.
The time you spend caring today will
be a love gift that will blossom into the
fresh joy of God's Spirit in the future.

EMILIE BARNES

APRIL 18

If instead of a gem,
or even a flower, we should cast
the gift of a loving thought into the
heart of a friend, that would be
giving as the angels give.

GEORGE MACDONALD

SEPTEMBER 14

I will send down showers in season; there will be showers of blessing.

EZEKIEL 34:26 NIV

APRIL 19

If you love someone, you will be loyal to them no matter what the cost.

1 CORINTHIANS 13:7 TLB

SEPTEMBER 13

*D*uty makes us do things well, but love makes us do them beautifully.

PHILLIPS BROOKS

APRIL 20

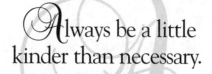

Always be a little
kinder than necessary.

JAMES M. BARRIE

SEPTEMBER 12

One who loves is borne on wings; she runs, and is filled with joy; she is free and unrestricted. She gives all to receive all, and she has all in all; for beyond all things she rests in the one highest thing, from Whom streams all that is good.

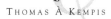

THOMAS À KEMPIS

APRIL 21

$\mathcal{W}$e have something precious.
I am reminded of that whenever
I am away from you, busy doing
something, and you drift into my
mind, making me smile inside.

GARRY LaFOLLETTE

SEPTEMBER 11

*I*n a world where it is necessary to succeed, perhaps...we women know more deeply that success can be a quiet and hidden thing.

PAM BROWN

APRIL 22

*Y*ou are valuable just because you exist. Not because of what you do or what you have done, but simply because you are.... Just think about the way Jesus honors you...and smile.

MAX LUCADO

SEPTEMBER 10

$\mathcal{B}$eauty is the radiance of truth, the fragrance of goodness.

VINCENT MCNABB

APRIL 23

*H*e shall give his angels charge over you, to keep you in all your ways. They shall bear you up in their hands, lest you dash your foot against a stone.

PSALM 91:11-12 NKJV

SEPTEMBER 9

*I*n response to all He has done for us, let us outdo each other in being helpful and kind to each other and in doing good.

HEBREWS 10:24 TLB

APRIL 24

$\mathcal{R}$ich is the woman who has a praying friend.

JANICE HUGHES

SEPTEMBER 8

The human heart,
at whatever age, opens
only to the heart that
opens in return.

❧

MARIA EDGEWORTH

APRIL 25

$\mathcal{G}$od...will take care
of you day and
night forever.

❦

DR. NORMAN VINCENT PEALE

SEPTEMBER 7

$\mathcal{Y}$ou will find as you look back upon your life that the moments when you have really lived are the moments when you have done things in the spirit of love.

HENRY DRUMMOND

APRIL 26

$\mathcal{T}$rue friendship comes when silence between two people is comfortable.

DAVE TYSON GENTRY

SEPTEMBER 6

*S*catter seeds of kindness everywhere
you go; scatter bits of courtesy—watch
them grow and grow. Gather buds of
friendship; keep them till full-blown;
you will find more happiness than
you have ever known.

AMY R. RAABE

APRIL 27

$\mathcal{A}$ shared secret
fosters intimacy.

JEAN FLEMING

SEPTEMBER 5

$\mathscr{Y}$ou can't give a
hug without getting
one in return.

❦

APRIL 28

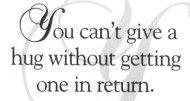

The Lord longs to be gracious to you; he rises to show you compassion. For the Lord is a God of justice. Blessed are all who wait for him!

❧

ISAIAH 30:18 NIV

SEPTEMBER 4

For, lo, the winter is past, the rain is over and gone; the flowers appear on the earth; the time of the singing of birds is come.

Song of Solomon 2:11,12 KJV

APRIL 29

*M*ake yourself
necessary to somebody.

RALPH WALDO EMERSON

SEPTEMBER 3

*L*ovely flowers are
the smiles of God's
goodness.

WILBERFORCE

APRIL 30

$\mathcal{P}$erhaps the most delightful friendships are those in which there is much agreement, much disputation, and yet more personal liking.

❦

GEORGE ELIOT

SEPTEMBER 2

The splendor of the rose and the whiteness of the lily do not rob the little violet of its scent nor the daisy of its simple charm. If every tiny flower wanted to be a rose, spring would lose its loveliness.

THERESE OF LISIEUX

MAY 1

God's gifts put man's best dreams to shame.

ELIZABETH BARRETT BROWNING

SEPTEMBER 1

*S*peak kind words
and you will hear
kind echoes.

❦

MAY 2

$\mathcal{W}$hatever you ask for in prayer, believe that you have received it, and it will be yours.

MARK 11:24 NIV

AUGUST 31

*M*ay you always be doing those good, kind things which show you are a child of God, for this will bring much praise and glory to the Lord.

PHILIPPIANS 1:11 TLB

MAY 3

*G*od's peace is joy
resting. His joy
is peace dancing.

❦

F. F. BRUCE

AUGUST 30

*L*ove is that condition
in which the happiness
of another person is
essential to your own.

ROBERT HEINLEIN

MAY 4

I know now that the world is not filled with strangers. It is full of other people—waiting only to be spoken to.

BETH DAY

AUGUST 29

$\mathcal{T}$ime is a very precious gift from God; so precious that it's only given to us moment by moment.

❧

AMELIA BARR

MAY 5

There is no soul that does not respond to love.

MAURICE MAETERLINCK

AUGUST 28

*L*aughing at ourselves
as well as with each
other gives a surprising
sense of togetherness.

HAZEL C. LEE

MAY 6

Treat your friends as you do your pictures, and place them in their best light.

JENNIE JEROME CHURCHILL

AUGUST 27

*T*he supreme happiness
of life is the conviction
that we are loved.

VICTOR HUGO

MAY 7

*S*o don't be anxious for tomorrow. God will take care of your tomorrow too. Live one day at a time.

MATTHEW 6:34 TLB

AUGUST 26

*T*rust in the Lord with all
your heart and lean not on your
own understanding; in all your
ways acknowledge him, and he
will make your paths straight.

PROVERBS 3:5,6 NIV

MAY 8

There is only one
happiness in life, to
love and be loved.

❧

GEORGE SAND

AUGUST 25

*L*ove is not the saying
of the words but the
giving of the self.

ROBERT LANDER

MAY 9

The essence of a perfect friendship is that each friend reveals herself utterly to the other, flings aside her reserves, and shows herself for what she truly is.

❧

ROBERT H. BENSON

AUGUST 24

$\mathcal{M}$any flowers open to the sun,
but only one follows it constantly.
Heart, be thou the sunflower, not
only open to receive God's blessing,
but constant in looking to Him.

JEAN PAUL RICHTER

MAY 10

*F*ill [your friends'] lives with sweetness. Speak approving, cheering words while their ears can hear them and while their hearts can be thrilled by them.

❧

HENRY WARD BEECHER

AUGUST 23

The really great person
is the one who makes
everyone feel great.

G. K. CHESTERTON

MAY 11

*D*on't be weary in prayer;
keep at it; watch for God's
answers, and remember to be
thankful when they come.

COLOSSIANS 4:2 TLB

AUGUST 22

Risky love
seizes the moment.

❧

MAX LUCADO

MAY 12

$\mathcal{L}$ife is God's gift to you. The way you live your life is your gift to God. Make it a fantastic one.

LEO BUSCAGLIA

AUGUST 21

*G*ive generously to him...
then because of this the
Lord your God will bless you in
all your work and in everything
you put your hand to.

❧

DEUTERONOMY 15:10 NIV

MAY 13

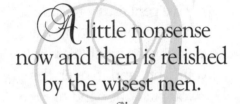

A little nonsense
now and then is relished
by the wisest men.

❦

AUGUST 20

$\mathcal{T}$he best things are nearest:
breath in your nostrils, light in
your eyes, flowers at your feet,
duties at your hand, the
path of God just before you.

ROBERT LOUIS STEVENSON

MAY 14

*I*nsomuch as anyone
pushes you nearer to God,
she is your truest friend.

AUGUST 19

$\mathcal{F}$riendships will last
if they are put first.

MAY 15

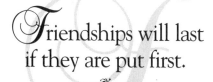

I said a prayer for you today and I know that God must have heard. I felt the answer in my heart.... I asked that He'd be near you at the start of each new day, grant you health and blessings.... It was for His loving care I prayed for most of all.

❦

AUGUST 18

I have found a paradox that if I love until it hurts, then there is no hurt, but only more love.

MOTHER TERESA

MAY 16

I know what it is to be in need, and I know what it is to have plenty. I have learned the secret of being content in any and every situation.

❧

PHILIPPIANS 4:12 NIV

AUGUST 17

Compassion means to lay a bridge over to the other without knowing whether she wants to be reached.

HENRI J. M. NOUWEN

MAY 17

*L*ove, to some extent,
protects you from age.

❧

JEANNE MOREAU

AUGUST 16

The Lord will guide you always; he will satisfy your needs.... You will be like a well-watered garden, like a spring whose waters never fail.

ISAIAH 58:11 NIV

MAY 18

$\mathscr{L}$ife in great abundance
comes only through
great love.

ELBERT HUBBARD

AUGUST 15

To feel love gives
pleasure to one; to express
it gives pleasure to two.

❧

JANETTE OKE

MAY 19

Everyone was meant to share
God's all-abiding love and care;
He saw that we would need to
know a way to let these feelings
show.... So God made hugs.

JILL WOLF

AUGUST 14

$\mathcal{W}$holehearted, ready laughter heals, encourages, relaxes anyone within hearing distance. The laughter that springs from love makes wide the space around it—gives room for the loved one to enter in.

EUGENIA PRICE

MAY 20

*F*inally...whatever is true,
whatever is noble, whatever is right,
whatever is pure, whatever is lovely,
whatever is admirable–if anything
is excellent or praiseworthy–
think about such things.

PHILIPPIANS 4:8 NIV

AUGUST 13

*L*ove comforteth like
sunshine after rain.

WILLIAM SHAKESPEARE

MAY 21

*G*ive what you have.
To someone it may
be better than you
dare to think.

AUGUST 12

*G*od walks with us.... He scoops us up in His arms or simply sits with us in silent strength until we cannot avoid the awesome recognition that yes, even now, He is here.

GLORIA GAITHER

MAY 22

*I*f we did the things we are capable of, we would astound ourselves.

❧

THOMAS EDISON

AUGUST 11

*G*od did not give us a spirit of timidity, but a spirit of power, of love and of self-discipline.

2 TIMOTHY 1:7 NIV

MAY 23

One cannot collect all the beautiful shells on the beach. One can collect only a few and they are more beautiful if they are few.

ANNE MORROW LINDBERGH

AUGUST 10

$\mathcal{W}$e are not called by God
to do extraordinary things,
but to do ordinary things
with extraordinary love.

❦

JEAN VANIER

MAY 24

$\mathcal{A}$ sister is a person who has a sneaky knack of saying good things about you behind your back.

AUGUST 9

*M*y sister often knows
the worst about me, but
she always believes in
the best!

MAY 25

*B*e full of sympathy
toward each other, loving
one another with tender
hearts and humble minds.

❧

1 PETER 3:8 TLB

AUGUST 8

When seeds of kindness are sown prayerfully in the garden plot of our lives, we may be sure that there will be a bountiful harvest of blessings for both us and others.

W. PHILLIP KELLER

MAY 26

$\mathcal{W}$e all mold one another's dreams. We all hold each other's fragile hopes in our hands. We all touch others' hearts.

❧

AUGUST 7

$\mathcal{I}$t is always springtime
in the heart that
loves God.

❧

JEAN-MARIE VIANNEY

MAY 27

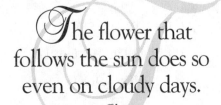

The flower that follows the sun does so even on cloudy days.

❧

AUGUST 6

*B*ecause the Lord is my
Shepherd, I have everything I need!
He lets me rest in the meadow grass
and leads me beside the quiet
streams. He gives me new strength.

PSALM 23:1-3 TLB

MAY 28

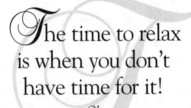

The time to relax
is when you don't
have time for it!

SYDNEY J. HARRIS

AUGUST 5

Today well lived makes every yesterday a dream of happiness and every tomorrow a vision of hope.

MAY 29

$\mathcal{B}$e beautiful inside, in
your hearts, with the lasting
charm of a gentle and quiet spirit
which is so precious to God.

1 PETER 3:4 TLB

AUGUST 4

*G*o where there
is no path and
leave a trail.

❦

MAY 30

It isn't great big pleasures that count the most; it's making a great deal out of the little ones.

JEAN WEBSTER

AUGUST 3

$\mathcal{L}$ive your life while you have it. Life is a splendid gift—there is nothing small about it.

❧

FLORENCE NIGHTINGALE

MAY 31

*L*aughter is the brush
that sweeps away the
cobwebs of the heart.

MORT WALKER

AUGUST 2

It is not who is right
that is of greatest
importance, but of
what is right.

❧

JUNE 1

*G*od loves and cares
for us, even to the
least event and smallest
need of life.

HENRY MANNING

AUGUST 1

$\mathcal{M}$ost smiles are started
by another smile.

❧

JUNE 2

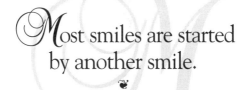

$\mathcal{W}$hatever your
hand finds to do, do it
with all your might.

ECCLESIASTES 9:10 NIV

JULY 31

No eye has seen, nor ear heard, nor the human heart conceived, what God has prepared for those who love him.

❧

1 CORINTHIANS 2:9 NRSV

JUNE 3

There is nothing more
magnetic or attractive
than your smile.

CHARLES R. SWINDOLL

JULY 30

*L*ove, consolation, and
peace bloom only in
the garden of sweet
contentment.

MARTHA ANDERSON

JUNE 4

The whole point
of getting things done
is knowing what to
leave undone.

❧

LADY STELLA READING

JULY 29

*P*eople live up to what
you believe of them.
Believe in the best!

❧

JUNE 5

Only visionaries can teach us to dream. Only realists can teach us to accomplish. We need both.

JULY 28

*T*he blossom cannot tell what becomes of its fragrance as it drifts away, just as no person can tell what becomes of their influence as they continue through life.

❧

JUNE 6

$\mathcal{A}$ great woman is
she who has not lost
the heart of a child.

MENCIUS

JULY 27

$\mathcal{T}$he best way to get
something done
is to begin.

❧

JUNE 7

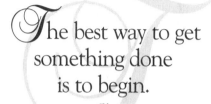

*L*ove the Lord your God with all your heart and with all your soul and with all your strength.

DEUTERONOMY 6:5 NIV

JULY 26

*G*od has given each of you some special abilities; be sure to use them to help each other, passing on to others God's many kinds of blessings.

❧

1 PETER 4:10 TLB

JUNE 8

*W*hat you do when you don't have to determines what you will be when you can no longer help it.

RUDYARD KIPLING

JULY 25

You'll learn more
about a road by traveling
it than by consulting all
the maps in the world.

❦

JUNE 9

$\mathcal{D}$etermine never to be idle.... It is wonderful how much may be done if we are always doing.

THOMAS JEFFERSON

JULY 24

Keep your ideals high enough to inspire you and low enough to encourage you.

JUNE 10

$\mathcal{W}$ith kindness, the difficult becomes easy...life assumes a charm and its miseries are softened.

CHARLES WAGER

JULY 23

*C*ease to inquire whatever
the future has in store, and
take as a gift whatever the
day brings forth.

HORACE

JUNE 11

*N*othing we can do will make
the Father love us less; nothing
we do can make Him love us more.
He loves us unconditionally with
an everlasting love.

❧

NANCIE CARMICHAEL

JULY 22

*N*o matter what you do...
God has a relentless,
undying, unfathomable,
unquenchable love.

❧

MAX LUCADO

JUNE 12

*D*o not withhold good
from those who deserve
it, when it is in your
power to act.

❧

PROVERBS 3:27 NIV

JULY 21

$\mathcal{L}$et him have all your
worries and cares, for he is always
thinking about you and watching
everything that concerns you.

1 PETER 5:7 TLB

JUNE 13

He is the God of the multitude and the God of the individual.... He will not overlook your tiniest need.

ROY LESSIN

JULY 20

*Y*ou are...infinitely dear to the Father, unspeakably precious to Him. You are never, not for one second, alone.

❦

NORMAN DOWTY

JUNE 14

Quarrels are like summer
storms. Everything is
more beautiful when
they have passed.

JULY 19

The real art of conversation
is not only to say the right
thing in the right place, but to
leave unsaid the wrong thing
at the tempting moment.

DOROTHY NEVILL

JUNE 15

*O*pportunities are often disguised as hard work, so most people don't recognize them.

ANN LANDERS

JULY 18

*W*hen a sincere
compliment comes to
mind, don't hesitate
to give it.

❧

JANETTE OKE

JUNE 16

*L*et love and faithfulness
never leave you; bind them
around your neck, write them
on the tablet of your heart.

PROVERBS 3:3 NIV

JULY 17

*W*henever you are asked
if you can do a job, tell them,
"Certainly I can!" Then get busy
and find out how to do it.

THEODORE ROOSEVELT

JUNE 17

*M*ay you wake each day with
His blessings and sleep each night
in His keeping, and may you
always walk in His tender care.

❧

JULY 16

*T*his is the confidence we have in approaching God: that if we ask anything according to his will, he hears us. And if we know that he hears us—whatever we ask—we know that we have what we asked of him.

1 JOHN 5:14,15 NIV

JUNE 18

What happens to you
is not as important as
how you react to
what happens.

*H*appiness held is the seed; happiness shared is the flower.

JUNE 19

*H*appiness is a sunbeam....
When it strikes a kindred heart, like
the converged lights upon a mirror, it
reflects itself with redoubled brightness.
It is not perfected until it is shared.

JANE PORTER

JULY 14

A wise person will
make more opportunities
than she finds.

❧

FRANCIS BACON

JUNE 20

*W*hat you would seem
to be, be really.

BENJAMIN FRANKLIN

JULY 13

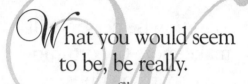

*L*ove is pressing around
us on all sides like air. Cease
to resist it and instantly
love takes possession.

AMY CARMICHAEL

JUNE 21

Wherever your treasure is, there your heart and thoughts will be also.

LUKE 12:34 TLB

JULY 12

$\mathcal{T}$ake time to be deliberate, but when the time for action has arrived, stop thinking and go in.

NAPOLEON BONAPARTE

JUNE 22

$\mathcal{W}$rite on your heart
that every day is the
best day of the year.

RALPH WALDO EMERSON

JULY 11

*A*nd God is able to
make all grace abound to you,
so that in all things at all times,
having all that you need, you will
abound in every good work.

2 CORINTHIANS 9:8 NIV

JUNE 23

The important thing is this:
To be ready at any moment to
sacrifice what we are for what
we could become.

CHARLES DUBOIS

JULY 10

*G*uard well your spare moments. They are like uncut diamonds. Discard them and their value will never be known. Improve them and they will become the brightest gems in useful life.

❧

RALPH WALDO EMERSON

JUNE 24

*H*old fast your dreams! Within your heart keep one still, secret spot where dreams may go and sheltered so, may thrive and grow.... O keep a place apart, within your heart, for little dreams to go!

LOUISE DRISCOLL

JULY 9

*Y*ou can take no credit for
beauty at sixteen. But if you
are beautiful at sixty, it will
be your soul's own doing.

❧

MARIE STOPES

JUNE 25

The journey of a thousand miles begins with a single step.

CHINESE PROVERB

JULY 8

$\mathcal{I}$f I had a single flower
for every time I think of
you, I could walk forever
in my garden.

❦

CLAUDIA A. GRANDI

JUNE 26

*Y*our heavenly Father
knows your needs. He will
always give you all you
need from day to day.

❧

LUKE 12:30,31 TLB

JULY 7

$\mathcal{A}$lthough we cannot change the direction of the wind, we can adjust the sails.

❧

JUNE 27

May God give you eyes
to see beauty only the
heart can understand.

JULY 6

*W*ithout God, it is utterly impossible. But with God everything is possible.

MARK 10:27 TLB

JUNE 28

*O*nly a life lived
for others is a life
worthwhile.

ALBERT EINSTEIN

JULY 5

Contentment is not the
fulfillment of what you want,
but the realization of how
much you already have.

JUNE 29

*W*e create opportunities
by seeing the possibilities and
having the persistence to act
upon them. We must remember...
opportunities are always here,
but we must look for them.

❧

JULY 4

*U*se what talents you possess:
the woods would be very silent
if no birds sang there except
those that sang best.

❦

HENRY VAN DYKE

JUNE 30

Tuck [this] thought into your heart today. Treasure it. Your Father God cares about your daily everythings that concern you.

❧

KAY ARTHUR

JULY 3

*W*ouldn't it be nice
if we could forget our
troubles as easily as we
forget our blessings?

❦

JULY 1

*I*t was God...who made
the garden grow in
your hearts.

❧

1 CORINTHIANS 3:6 TLB

JULY 2